University Meets Microfinance

Partners

In Collaboration with:

- Université Libre de Bruxelles / Belgium
- ESCEM / France
- ESC Dijon / France
- Sciences Po / France
- Freie Universität Berlin / Germany
- Leibniz Universität Hannover / Germany
- Eberhard Karls Universität Tübingen / Germany
- Rijksuniversiteit Groningen / The Netherlands
- Frankfurt School of Finance and Management / Germany
- Università Cattolica del Sacro Cuore Milano / Italy
- Università degli Studi di Bergamo / Italy
- Università degli Studi di Roma "La Sapienza" / Italy
- Universidade Católica Portuguesa / Portugal
- Universidade Nova de Lisboa / Portugal
- European Microfinance Platform (e-MFP)

We thank the following professors and practitioners for having participated in the Selection Committee: Ashta Arvind (ESC Dijon), Diego Dagradi and Maria Cristina Negro (Fondazione Giordano Dell'Amore), Marie-Anne de Villepin (BNP Paribas), Oliver Gloede (Leibniz University Hannover), Philippe Guichandut (Grameen Crédit Agricole), Hansjorg Leo Kessler (FIDES), Katja Kirchstein (Freie Universität Berlin), Thilo Klein (University of Cambridge), Roland Knorren (ACCION), Julien Lacombe (Microcred), Christina May (Universität Köln), Klaas Molenaar and Julie-Marthe Lehmann (INHolland) Margherita Mori (Università degli Studi dell' Aquila), Roberto Moro Visconti (Università Cattolica del Sacro Cuore), Ahmad Nawaz (Universität Göttingen), Lucia Poletti (Università degli Studi di Parma), Marie Pons, Vincenzo Provenzano (Università degli Studi di Palermo), Jessica Schicks (Université Libre de Bruxelles), Baptiste Venet (Université Paris Dauphine), Laura Viganò and Davide Castellani (Università degli studi di Bergamo) as well as Eliane Augareils, Delphine Bazalgette, Pauline Bensoussan, Maud Chalamet, Frances Fraser, Gabrielle Harris, Miquel Jordana and Vanessa Quintero (PlaNet Finance).

With the Financial Support of:

escem SOGETI **BOMBARDIER** The Global Leader in Rail Technology ERNST & YOUNG Quality In Everything We Do Capgemini CONSULTING TECHNOLOGY OUTSOURCING sanofi aventis

With Kind Support of:

Allianz SE, BNP Paribas, Frankfurt School of Finance and Management and Dexia Kommunalbank Deutschland AG supported UMM activities (workshop, scholarship)

Collaboration with European Microfinance Platform

In 2010 the European Microfinance Platform (e-MFP) has set up an e-MFP Action Group "University Meets Microfinance" for practitioners to work with European universities and further enhance students´ research and microfinance professionalization.

EUROPEAN
MICROFINANCE
PLATFORM
NETWORKING WITH THE SOUTH

UNIVERSITY MEETS MICROFINANCE

edited by PlaNet Finance Deutschland e.V.

ISSN 2190-2291

The "University Meets Microfinance" Programme (UMM) presents its eighth "UMM Award": Each year the UMM Awards honour outstanding theses on microfinance and give recognition to the work of young researchers. The UMM Award winners are selected by a committee of professors and microfinance practitioners, to recognize these presenting innovative research topics and approaches.

Microfinance has gained scale and recognition over the last decade. Today, Microfinance Institutions reach approximately 190 million low-income people, who were previously excluded from formal banking systems, with financial services which include credit, savings, insurance and money transfer. This rapid expansion has also come with increasing challenges.

Research on microfinance provides new insights into these challenges and can foster innovation in the sector.

As of today UMM events gathered 1886 students, professors and practitioners from 10 European countries. The Programme is co-financed by the European Union and was initiated by PlaNet Finance and Freie Universität Berlin with the aim of strengthening the cooperation between European universities and microfinance practitioners. In addition to promoting research publications, UMM offers microfinance seminars in partnership with European universities, mentorship and field research scholarship for Bachelor, Master and PhD students and organizes regular workshops with UMM participants.

More information can be found at
www.universitymeetsmicrofinance.eu and www.planetfinance.org

Volumes

Anna Custers

FURTHERING FINANCIAL LITERACY:

Experimental Evidence from a Financial Literacy
Training Programme for Microfinance Clients
in Bhopal, India

ibidem-Verlag
Stuttgart

Bibliografische Information der Deutschen Nationalbibliothek
Die Deutsche Nationalbibliothek verzeichnet diese Publikation in der
Deutschen Nationalbibliografie; detaillierte bibliografische Daten sind im
Internet über http://dnb.d-nb.de abrufbar.

Bibliographic information published by the Deutsche Nationalbibliothek
Die Deutsche Nationalbibliothek lists this publication in the Deutsche Nationalbibliografie;
detailed bibliographic data are available in the Internet at http://dnb.d-nb.de.

∞

Gedruckt auf alterungsbeständigem, säurefreien Papier
Printed on acid-free paper

ISSN: 2190-2291

ISBN-13: 978-3-8382-0337-9

© *ibidem*-Verlag
Stuttgart 2012

Printed in Germany

Abstract

This study presents evidence from a randomised field experiment that was conducted in Bhopal, India. It investigates the effects of a financial literacy training programme on the financial literacy levels of microfinance clients. This study found that there was a significant positive impact on financial literacy levels due to the training. In addition, it tests whether trainer gender influences the impact of the training. It does this by looking at the learning outcomes and learning perceptions, for which no or little significant causality was found, respectively. The sample for the experiment was drawn from a local microfinance organisation that caters to women in the state of Madhya Pradesh.

and implicit incentives of the microfinance programmes themselves, or if they result instead from the poor financial literacy of microfinance clients. Understanding these dynamics could suggest starkly different policy responses.

An active strand in the literature on microfinance has taken shape around two main themes: understanding the impact of financial literacy on microfinance outcomes and identifying the best strategies on how to improve the financial literacy of the poor. This study represents an important part of this emerging literature. Its main goal is to apply rigorous experimental methods to understand whether a financial literacy programme affects the levels of financial literacy of microfinance clients. It then goes one step further to also test the impact of different methods of delivering the literacy programme on both learning outcomes and perceptions of learning among microfinance recipients. An extensive literature in science education has grappled with the role played by the gender of the instructor on actual and perceived learning outcomes. This study represents one of the first to apply experimental methods to directly test for the importance of the gender of the instructor in the context of financial literacy programmes. This is particularly relevant in an environment that is not gender neutral, given that the majority of microfinance clients are female.

We are still far from understanding exactly how, and to what extent, the microfinance promise can be fulfilled. The financial literacy of microfinance clients appears to be a fundamental piece of this puzzle. Rigorous studies that attempt to identify how to maximize its potential represent an important step in the right direction.

Sandra Sequeira, London, 2011

Editorial

Microfinance programmes have flourished in recent decades, hailed as an innovative means of bringing much needed financial resources to the poor. These programmes attract significant volumes of both private and philanthropic capital worldwide, with over 100 million households throughout the developing world reporting to have already received some form of micro-loan. The enthusiasm surrounding microfinance has however been dampened by recent reports of over-zealous loan repayment officers seeking to maintain high repayment rates at any cost, soaring interest rates that have begun to match the shark loan lending rates microfinance was designed to replace, and overly indebted households consistently failing to make ends meet. As the political backlash against microfinance grew in scale and intensity, the development industry began to rethink the role, if any, microfinance programmes could play in development. Governments at the epicentre of the crisis began to actively intervene in the industry, either through heavy regulation or outright bans of microfinance operations. This sudden change of heart was in part driven by the lack of rigorous evidence on the impact microfinance programmes were in fact having on the poor.

Since the crisis emerged, new studies applying rigorous experimental and quasi-experimental methods started to paint a more nuanced picture of the real impact of microfinance. In some cases microfinance programmes seem to have provided much needed business capital but for those with the right traits to become entrepreneurs. Other studies focused on indirect benefits such as the fact that regular microfinance meetings could generate new sources of social capital. The most worrisome cases were however those in which microfinance programmes led to cycles of over-borrowing, with households struggling under the weight of unmanageable debt.

A central question in this debate is whether these instances of over-borrowing and mismanagement of loans are a direct result of the structure

Acknowledgements

First and foremost, I would like to thank Praseeda Kunam and Bala Krishnamurthy, and all the other people working at Samhita Community Development Services and eCubeH Research Labs for their exceptional support in making the randomised field experiment upon which this study is based possible.

Special thanks also go to Dr Sandra Sequeira from the London School of Economics for her continuous support, guidance and motivation throughout the year.

Table of Contents

1. Introduction

Improving of individual financial skills has been receiving increasing attention both in the developed and developing world. In late 2006, the government of the Netherlands, in cooperation with the Dutch Central Bank, universities and several NGOs, introduced an online platform for helping consumers become more financially self-sufficient[1]. Similar projects have been launched around the world. The Reserve Bank of India, for example, started financial literacy initiatives in late 2007, which consisted of a financial education website and free financial education and counselling for various target groups.[2] With 2010 being declared the year of financial inclusion by the G20's Financial Inclusion Experts Group, the question of how to develop financial literacy seems more pertinent than ever.

The idea behind the efforts to improve financial literacy is that it helps households make better-informed choices by demanding sound financial services which, in turn, are believed to increase their well-being. This idea is motivated by a compelling body of evidence that shows a strong association between financial literacy and a household's well-being (Cole et al., 2009:3). In particular, financial literacy training can help prevent problems, such as cycle lending and other forms of financial market participation that are not beneficial. In addition, it could increase demand for welfare enhancing financial services like savings accounts and pensions.

This study analyses the role of financial literacy in the demand for financial services by implementing a randomised field experiment focussing on a financial literacy training programme (FLTP) for microfinance clients in Bhopal, India. It compares individuals who received financial literacy training to individuals who did not receive training, but who closely

---

[1] See http://www.wijzeringeldzaken.nl/english.aspx.
[2] See http://www.rbi.org.in/scripts/PublicationDraftReports.aspx?ID=526.

resemble the first group. The FLTP was implemented by Samhita Micro-finance, a microfinance organisation that caters to women in the state of Madhya Pradesh.

A randomised evaluation is considered to give one of the most unbiased impact assessments of all research methods available.[3] It minimises biases due to omitted variables, selection bias and reverse causality and is believed to produce the optimum counterfactual inference (Duflo et al., 2006). This method strongly echoes Przeworski's view that counterfactual observations are required for inferring causal relationships (Przeworski, 2004:536). Moreover, a randomised field experiment does not only measure impact, but also departs from a theoretical framework and subsequently tests this theory in the field. It thus goes beyond a mere programme evaluation (Duflo et al., 2006:22).

The aim of this study is to make a two-fold contribution to the theory of financial literacy. Firstly, the study departs from the theoretical discussion surrounding financial literacy by focussing on a specific link in the theoretical mechanism between financial literacy and household well-being, which is the connection between financial literacy training and financial literacy levels. This link is tested in the field. The study does this by asking whether an FLTP affects the financial literacy levels of microfinance clients.

Secondly, again departing from theory, this study tests how trainer gender may affect learning outcomes and perceptions. This is a relatively under-researched field, in particular, in the context of developing countries. The way the study tests how learning outcomes and perceptions are affected by trainer gender is y asking whether a differential design of an FLTP, based on trainer gender, affects the financial literacy levels and learning perceptions of microfinance clients differently.

---

[3]   For a discussion of this methodology, see Ravaillon (2009) and Rodrik (2008).

This study reports the following main findings: Firstly, it finds a significant positive effect on financial literacy levels as a result of the FLTP. Secondly, it finds no or little significant causality between trainer gender and learning outcomes and perceptions, respectively. These results are outlined in more detail in the concluding sections of this study.

This study is structured as follows: The next section discusses the two theoretical departures for the randomised evaluation and introduces the three research questions following from this. Section 3 then discusses the empirical setting and research design. Section 4 focuses on measurements and section 5 outlines the sample selection and provides a test of randomisation. In section 6, departures from perfect randomisation are discussed, including the possible biases itintroduced in the results. Section 7 further outlines the results, which are subsequently discussed in section 8. Section 9 concludes the study.

2. Theoretical Framework and Research Questions

This section presents the theoretical discussion that informs the randomised field experiment. The first part discusses the theoretical debate surrounding financial literacy and the second part discusses the theoretical motivation behind the trainer gender experiment within the FLTP.

2.1 Financial Market Participation Theories

Limited access to, or limited use of financial services generates persistent poverty traps. In that way, financial exclusion can act as a hindrance to economic development (Demirgüç-Kunt et al., 2007:22; Beck, Demirgüç-Kunt, 2008:384). Financial exclusion can either be voluntarily chosen or involuntarily suffered. In the case of involuntary exclusion, access is always restricted and supply fails to meet demand (Claessens, 2006:211). In the case of voluntary exclusion, using financial services is not restricted by availability, but by low levels of demand.[4] This problem is particularly evident in developing countries. In many instances, formal financial markets are emerging quickly in developing countries, yet demand remains limited, in particular among the poor (ATISG, 2010).

Broadly speaking, two types of explanations have been offered to explain the low levels of demand. One view argues that these services are often still too costly for the poor in terms of transaction costs. For example, opening a savings account could involve a significant investment of time, especially if traveling to the bank is required. In other words, formal financial participation can be hindered by external cost constraints. An alternative explanation is that demand for financial services is low due to limited awareness or limited financial literacy. If individuals lack knowledge of financial products, there will simply be little demand for them (Cole et al.,

---

[4]   The classification of the reasons for exclusion used in this paper is based upon Claessens (2006) and Kempson et al. (2000).

2009:1; Kempson et al., 2000:50). According to this view, formal participation is hindered by internal cognitive constraints.

These two explanations imply quite different policy options for increasing the demand for financial services. On the one hand, reducing external constraints, such as transaction costs, for example via subsidies, could increase demand. On the other hand, reducing internal cognitive constraints via an FLTP could also increase demand. Cole et al. (2009:5) were the first to test these two competing theories in a developing country by conducting a randomised field experiment among unbanked households in Indonesia. The authors found that for the population at large, small subsidy payments had a significant impact on the likelihood of opening a savings account, whereas an FLTP did not.[5] However, they did find that the training programme had a modest impact on relatively uneducated and financially illiterate households, in terms of opening savings accounts. Nevertheless, their results suggest that the poor are held back more by external than internal factors, such as limited accessibility because saving products are too expensive.

Given the attention that policymakers pay to financial literacy training, these results are remarkable. They call into question the commonly assumed causal mechanism between financial literacy training and improved household well-being. This causal mechanism can be depicted as follows:

Financial Literacy Training → Financial Literacy Level ⇑ → Demand Welfare Enhancing Financial Services ⇑
→ Household Well-Being ⇑

Source: Own Compilation

Cole et al. (2009) focus on this causal mechanism between financial literacy training and the demand for welfare enhancing services (measured by

---

[5] A savings account is regarded as a sound indicator of financial market participation, as this is generally the first service that people take up when they enter the formal financial market (ATISG, 2010:11).

the opening up of a savings account), but do not measure the direct impact of a training programme on financial literacy levels. Cole et al. (2009) explore financial literacy levels before the intervention, but do not conduct a post-measurement of financial literacy levels. It is therefore unclear whether the authors found that the financial literacy training had no effect on the demand for savings accounts because it did not increase financial literacy levels, or because increased financial literacy levels did not result in a higher demand for savings accounts. In other words, it is possible that financial literacy levels increased without this translating into a higher demand for savings accounts. This point will be elaborated on in the discussion.

This study builds upon the findings of Cole et al. (2009) by investigating the link between financial literacy training and financial literacy levels. It focuses on the determinants of low demand for financial services due to internal cognitive constraints. To do so, it asks research question 1:

1) Does a financial literacy training programme affect financial literacy levels among microfinance clients in Bhopal, India?

To answer this question, this study makes use of a randomised field experiment, in which microfinance clients are randomly assigned to an FLTP or a control group. Section 3.2.1 describes this experiment in more detail.

2.2 Teacher Gender Theories

In addition to testing the effect of an FLTP on financial literacy levels, this study investigates whether teacher gender status has any effect on the training programme. Samhita Microfinance has a preference for female trainers because they believe women make better trainers for an all-female clientele. It is a common assumption that male and female teachers have different teaching styles and capacities which may influence students in different ways (Sabbe & Aelterman, 2007:521).

The literature on the effects of teacher gender provides at least two theories of how it may affect learning outcomes and perceptions. One view suggests that self-recognition plays an important role in learning. According to this view, women develop more positive attitudes towards traditionally non-female subjects, such as mathematics, when it is taught by a female (Li, 1999). An alternative view suggests that the perception of authority regarding the subject being studied differs by subject and gender. In particular, mathematics is often stereotyped as a male domain (Li, 1999).

These two theories suggest a differential design of financial literacy training for female clients. On the one hand, hiring female trainers could result in better learning outcomes and in a better perception of the training because a female trainer makes the female clients feel more comfortable, for example, in asking questions. On the other hand, hiring male trainers could give better results. In this case, the female clients may perceive men as more knowledgeable on the subject, or as better teachers in terms of leadership.

The effect of gender in teaching is relatively well researched. Sabbe and Aelterman (2007) have provided a comprehensive overview of this research to date. One of their findings is that gender has little, if any, effect on learning outcomes (Ibid., 526). They do find some evidence that teacher gender affects learning perceptions (Ibid., 527). However, the vast majority of the research on gender in teaching has been conducted in developed countries (Warwick & Jatoi, 1994:377). There has not been much research done with respect to similar effects in a development context, in particular with regard to financial literacy training. This probably has to do with the fact that financial literacy is a new practice.

Given the above, it is relevant to test Samhita's FLTP with respect to the effects of trainer gender on learning outcomes and perceptions. This is done on the basis of research questions 2a and 2b below:

2a) Does a differential design of a financial literacy training programme, based on trainer gender, affect the financial literacy levels of microfinance clients in Bhopal, India differently?

2b) Does a differential design of a financial literacy training programme, based on trainer gender, affect the perceptions of the training programme in Bhopal, India differently?

In answering these questions, this study randomly allocates comparable male and female trainers to a comparable subgroup of clients that is receiving financial literacy training. Section 3.2.2 describes the trainer gender experiment focussing on financial literacy levels in more detail. In addition, this study analyses trainer evaluations in order to determine whether learning perceptions vary according to trainer gender. The trainer evaluation is discussed in section 4.

3. Empirical Setting and Experiment Design

This section describes the FLTP offered to microfinance clients in Bhopal. It subsequently describes the parameters of the field experiment and the empirical research strategy.

3.1 Empirical Setting: Samhita Microfinance and its Financial Literacy Training Programme

To study whether financial literacy training could affect financial literacy levels, I had the opportunity to work with Samhita Microfinance. Samhita is a non-profit, financially sustainable microfinance institution, which has been operating in Madhya Pradesh (MP), India since September 2007. The state ranks among the eight poorest in India, as measured by the multidimensional poverty index, and is the sole Indian state that falls into the 'extremely alarming' category of the India State Hunger Index (UNDP, 2010; Menon et al., 2009). Samhita's microfinance model is based upon that of Bangladesh's Grameen Bank, with lending groups of five individuals.[6] Four to five of these types of lending groups usually form a centre, which meet for weekly loan repayments. Samhita accepts only female clients.

Samhita's mission is to provide community development services that go beyond providing credit. Its financial literacy programme is such a service. The goal of the training is to empower clients in their financial decision making. For this purpose, Samhita developed a customised financial literacy training for its urban clients in Bhopal, which consisted of the following four sessions: budgeting, savings and investments, insurances and loans, and a recap session. The training was tailored to people with a low level of literacy and relied heavily on pictorial and interactive training materials, including a movie.[7]

---

[6] For a more detailed description of this model, see Murdoch (1999).
[7] 48% of its targeted audience was illiterate (Source: baseline survey).

3.2 Field Experiment Design: Financial Literacy Intervention and Trainer Gender Experiment

3.2.1 Financial Literacy Intervention

The evaluation of Samhita's financial literacy training was conducted by means of a randomised phase-in experiment that took place during a field visit in July 2010. A randomised phase-in experiment is considered one of the fairest field experiment varieties within the method of randomised evaluation, since ultimately all eligible beneficiaries will receive the intervention (Duflo et al., 2006:25). The clients selected for treatment received two weekly sessions of two hours for a period of two weeks. The randomisation was based upon a baseline survey that was conducted by a professional team as part of Samhita's FLTP between March and May 2010. Out of 9,940 clients, the baseline survey covered 9,195 clients. The members included in the baseline survey were a random subset of Samhita's Bhopal client population. None of the branches were excluded beforehand, however, some clients were left out due to repeated unavailability at the time of the survey.

In order to ensure the internal validity of the results, the treatment and control groups have to be comparable prior to the intervention, in particular with regard to those characteristics that are likely to have a high correlation with the potential to change financial literacy levels. From the baseline survey, three indicators were chosen to form the basis of the randomisation.[8] In order of importance, they are as follows:

---

[8]   The indicators are not exhaustive in this respect, however, they are considered to be of primary importance. Other plausible indicators for the randomisation could be wealth, literacy levels, household size and other financial services uptake. See also Cole et al. (2009). These indicators were included in the checks of randomisation once treatment and control group selection had taken place.

1. Years of Schooling

Theory suggests that higher human capital, in particular higher cognitive ability, is strongly associated with financial literacy (Cole et al., 2009:12). In the absence of a direct measurement of cognitive ability, following current academic practice, I use years of schooling as a proxy for human capital.[9]

2. Whether a client has a savings account in her name

A savings account is regarded as a sound indicator for financial market participation because it is generally the first service that people take up when entering the formal financial market (ATISG, 2010:11). Having a savings account is likely to affect initial financial literacy levels, and also has the potential to increase financial literacy levels, due to familiarity with the subject matter.

3. Age

In their analysis of what predicts financial literacy, Cole et al. (2009:33) found that age (squared) had a significant effect on the financial literacy scores. A possible explanation for this is that financial participation (and therefore financial literacy scores) varies with age. When testing this hypothesis, Cole et al. (2009:34) found that age is only a significant predictor for formal loans. However, even if women themselves do not participate in the financial market, others in their families might (this varies according to age, e.g., when women marry or their children grow up), which may, in turn, influence their financial literacy levels. Therefore, I decided to select age as one of the main three indicators for the randomisation.

---

[9] This has long been accepted as a good proxy, but the academic debate in this field is far from settled (Cohen & Soto, 2007:52). For the purpose of this paper, however, years of schooling seems to be an adequate indicator – and in fact the only one available – of educational attainment.

In addition, both groups would ideally have a similar variation in initial financial literacy levels prior to the intervention. The baseline survey, however, does not contain a pre-measurement of financial literacy.[10] Nevertheless, the three indicators chosen as the basis for the randomisation can be considered accurate predictors of initial financial literacy levels; and are therefore considered to produce comparable groups with respect to initial financial literacy level variation as well.

3.2.2 Trainer Gender Experiment

In addition to the financial literacy intervention, I had the opportunity to study whether trainer gender affects the financial literacy levels or perceptions of the training. This was done by randomly allocating male and female trainers to comparable treatment groups. Working with Samhita enabled the identification of four comparable trainers of both sexes. All trainers were similar in terms of age and education, as well as working and teaching experience. The two more experienced trainers (male and female) were matched, as were the two younger trainers (male and female). Both couples were scheduled to train comparable treatment groups, making gender the most pertinent factor of variation.

3.3 Empirical Strategy and Data Collection

The empirical strategy of this study is to compare the average financial literacy levels of clients that have received financial literacy training to those who have not yet received the training. When assignment to the treatment and control group is randomly determined and correctly implemented, the unbiased causal effect of the financial literacy intervention can be obtained by estimating the following simple specification[11]:

---

[10]   This is often the case in educational interventions, when pre-measurements of educational attainment only take place after the randomisation (see for example Banerjee et al., 2005).

[11]   This equation can be estimated with ordinary least squares (see also Duflo et al., 2006:8).

$$FinLiteracy_i = \alpha + \beta * LitTraining + \varepsilon_i \tag{1}$$

Where $FinLiteracy_i$ is the average financial literacy level for client i after the training, and $LitTraining$ is a dummy for assignment to the financial literacy training (i.e., the treatment group).

In addition, this study compares the average financial literacy levels of clients that have received financial literacy training by a female trainer to those who have been trained by a male trainer. When assignment to a female and male trainer is randomly determined and correctly followed, the unbiased causal effect of the trainer gender experiment can be obtained by estimating the following simple specification[12]:

$$FinLiteracy_i = \alpha + \beta * FemaleTrainer + \varepsilon_i \tag{2}$$

Where $FinLiteracy_i$ is the average financial literacy level for client i after the training, and $FemaleTrainer$ is a dummy for assignment to a female trainer.

To measure the effect of the financial literacy intervention on the average financial literacy levels, original data collection for the purpose of this study took place during a field visit in July 2010. Pre-tests and post-tests, were given to measure the financial literacy levels of the treatment and control groups before and after the financial literacy intervention. To evaluate whether trainer gender could affect the perceptions of the training, this study makes use of a trainer evaluation that was part of the post-tests. The following section describes these surveys in more detail.

---

[12] Ibid.

4. Measuring Financial Literacy and Trainer Gender Perceptions

In their seminal paper on *'Financial Literacy and Planning'*, Lusardi and Mitchell (2006) introduced three questions on financial literacy into the nationally representative U.S. Health and Retirement Study, in order to measure the financial literacy levels of Americans over the age of 50. In recent years, these questions have become the standard measure of financial literacy levels. They have been extended to different target audiences and different countries. For example, the same questions have been adopted to measure financial literacy among American youth (Lusardi et al., 2009) and Dutch households (Van Rooij et al., 2009). Using the same approach, Cole et al. (2009) were the first to explore financial literacy levels in the context of a developing country for Indonesia and India.

4.1 Financial Literacy Survey

The pre-test and post-test contained four questions on financial literacy. These included the three standardised questions as originally developed by Lusardi and Mitchell (2006), which were adapted to an Indian context by Cole et al. (2009). The questions refer to basic fundamental financial concepts, such as compound interest rate calculation, inflation, and risk diversification (Lusardi and Mitchell, 2006:5). The following two questions were adopted verbatim from Cole et al. (2009:7–8):

i. 'Suppose you borrow Rs. 100 from a moneylender at an interest rate of 2 percent per month, with no repayment for three months. After three months, do you owe less than Rs. 102, exactly Rs. 102, or more than Rs. 102?'

ii. 'Suppose you have Rs. 100 in a savings account earning 1% interest per year. Over the period of a year, the prices for goods and services rise 2%. With the money in your savings account, can you buy more than, less than, or the same amount of goods in one year as you could today?'

The third question asked by Cole et al. (2009:8) was: 'Is it riskier to plant multiple crops or one crop?'[13] Since the sample of this study concerns an urban, rather than rural population, I decided to adapt this question to an urban context. In consultation with Samhita, the question was adapted as follows:

iii. If you had Rs. 1000 would you put it in a bank that will pay you Rs. 1100 after a year or would you give it to an agent of a scheme who will give you Rs. 2000 after a year?

Inevitably, this formulation has altered the nature of the question from risk diversification to risk aversion. Nevertheless, the specific amounts were chosen in order to make the second option represent a highly dubious financial investment. Choosing the second option, would therefore imply lower financial literacy since it would be unlikely to improve a household's financial well-being.

In addition to these three standardised questions, Cole et al. (2009) developed a fourth question regarding simple interest calculation. This question was adopted verbatim in the survey (Cole et al., 2009:8):

iv. 'Suppose you need to borrow Rs. 500. Two people offer you a loan. One loan requires you to pay back Rs. 600 in one month. The second loan requires you to pay back in one month Rs. 500 plus 15% interest. Which loan represents a better deal for you?'

---

[13] Cole et al. have translated the question by Lusardi and Mitchell (2006) to fit an Indian context. The original question by Lusardi and Mitchell (2006:5) is: 'Do you think that the following statement is true or false? "Buying a single company stock usually provides a safer return than a stock in a mutual fund." '

4.2 Trainer Evaluation

In the last training session, participants were asked to evaluate their trainer by means of a trainer evaluation. Besides covering questions on the general perceptions of the training, such as training material and group dynamics, four questions were asked that specifically related to trainer gender perceptions. Responses to these four questions form the basis of the analysis for research question 2b, which explores how trainer gender may affect learning perceptions.

More specifically, the following two questions were asked in order to evaluate the importance of self-recognition and class comfort:

i) How well did you think the trainer understood your specific needs in the programme?

Very well   Well   Average   Not so well   Poorly

ii) How comfortable did you feel with asking questions in class?

Very Comfortable   Comfortable   Somewhat Comfortable
Not very Comfortable   Not at all Comfortable

In order to evaluate the perceptions related to subject authority, the following two questions were asked:

iii) Please rate the instructor's teaching and leadership (circle one)

Excellent   Good   Average   Fair   Poor

iv) Please rate the instructor's knowledge for today's training (circle one)

Excellent   Good   Average   Fair   Poor

5. Sample Selection and Test of Randomisation

This section describes the experimental sample selection that formed the basis of the randomised field experiment. In addition, it provides a test of randomisation.

5.1 Experimental Sample Selection and Randomisation

The randomised phase-in experiment was carried out within Samhita's logistical constraints. Branch selection for training is assumed largely exogenous to the clients' (potential to improve) initial financial literacy levels: Two out of five branches were selected for implementation of the field experiment: Arera Colony and Nehru Nagar. These branches were selected because of their proximity to the head office. Both branches are considered large and mature according to Samhita's branch classification, and are comparable in terms of years in operation. This precludes any bias due to the length of time of a client's affiliation with Samhita. This is supported by the average number of loan clients in these two branches: comparing means using a t-test assuming unequal variances gives a p-value of 0.50353.[14] The two branches are also largely comparable in terms of the number of loan clients: In June 2010, Arera Colony had 2,468 loan clients, compared to 1,926 in Nehru Nagar.

5.1.1 Treatment Group Selection

Within the two branches, clients were invited to participate in the FLTP at the centre level. The availability of training locations, clients and times of the weekly centre meeting determined which centres were invited to the financial literacy training first. One of Samhita's employees was asked to pick the centres for training, without having any prior knowledge of the randomised field experiment that would be implemented.

---

[14] The p-value reported here refers to the experimental sample as described in this section. An ideal sample would have consisted of all the loan clients of these two branches.

This approach raises possible concerns regarding endogeneity. When treatment centres are systematically picked on the basis of (the potential to increase) financial literacy levels, the results may be biased. However, in the case of this field experiment, a programme timing bias does not seem to be a major concern. The availability of a large pool of potential control groups allowed control groups that were very similar in all main baseline characteristics to be randomly picked, as described in section 3. Thus, even when treatment group selection was not perfectly random, but rather determined by Samhita's logistical constraints, control group selection *was* random. This approach ensures the internal validity of the results because it prevents a bias arising due to the non-comparability of the treatment and control groups prior to the intervention. It may, however, affect the external validity of the experiment when the selected sample is no longer representative for the population of Samhita's 10,000 urban loan clients. This is discussed further in section 8.

The final treatment group selection resulted in 17 client clusters for training – 9 of these clusters were in the Arera Colony branch and 8 were in the Nehru Nagar branch. Each cluster consisted of 2 or more centres based upon matching weekly centre meetings. Over-sampling took place, as it was expected that not all clients would be instantly available. In Arera Colony, this resulted in a total of 22 centres being selected for treatment, compared to 23 centres in Nehru Nagar. This resulted in a sample of 501 clients for treatment. These clients were invited to participate in the FLTP.

By chance, the treatment groups both within Arera Colony and Nehru Nagar could be matched in pairs, which were very similar in terms of the three main baseline indicators: education, savings account and age.[15]

---

[15]   Due to the odd number of treatment groups in Arera Colony, one group was left out. This resulted in a sample of 469 for the trainer gender analysis.

This allowed for the random allocation of male and female trainers among the comparable treatment groups.[16]

5.1.2 Control Group Selection

Control groups for Arera Colony and Nehru Nagar were picked separately, in order to achieve optimum comparability of treatment and control groups. For each branch, a slightly different approach was taken with regard to control group selection. In Nehru Nagar, the 152 centres that were left after the treatment groups were selected were regrouped into similar 'potential training' groups based on weekly centre meetings. This resulted in ideal control groups since it was these combinations that Samhita would use when scheduling the financial literacy training. The exercise resulted in 64 potential control groups for Nehru Nagar. These 64 potential control groups were then compared to the treatment group according to the three main baseline indicators. For each treatment group, two or three comparable control groups were identified depending on the indicator variation. The actual control groups were subsequently selected by using Microsoft Excel's unique random number generator.[17] This generated four control groups in Nehru Nagar comprised of 8 centres and 98 clients.

Due to logistical constraints, centres could not be regrouped as per weekly centre meetings for control group selection in Arera Colony. Instead, the centres were considered at the randomisation level. This resulted in 166 potential control group centres.[18] Subsequently, following a similar approach for control group selection as in Nehru Nagar resulted in five control groups in Arera Colony comprised of 5 centres and 68 clients.

---

[16] For every pair, a number between one and two was randomly generated, using Microsoft Excel's unique random number generator. Using the third draw, a one resulted in a female trainer, and a two resulted in a male trainer.

[17] For every cluster of comparable control groups, a number between 1 and 3 (2) was randomly generated. After the third draw, the group receiving number two was picked as a control group.

[18] Out of 173 centers, 7 centers had to be dropped due to missing baseline data or size (smaller than 6).

In total, of 9,940 potential beneficiaries, an experimental sample of 667 clients was randomly selected for treatment (501) and control groups (166).

5.2 Key Descriptive Statistics and Test of Randomisation

This section reports the summary statistics for the experimental sample. In addition, it provides a test of randomisation. All statistics refer to the experimental sample as described in the previous subsection.

The experimental sample in this study concerns female microfinance clients in an urban setting. The baseline survey reveals that the average age of the women is 34 (SD 8.0). The distribution of years of schooling is very skewed: 49.6% have not had any education at all, whereas of those having attended school, 68% have completed the fifth grade or higher and 56% have completed the eighth grade or higher. The literacy levels reflect these figures: 52% of the women reported that they were able to read and write.

The summary statistics on the use of financial services prior to the training is presented in Table 1. Since the experimental sample is composed of microfinance clients, every person has at least one loan in her name. In addition, they each hold a life insurance through Samhita, which covers the original loan amount over the course of a year.

Summary Statistics Experimental Sample	
Loan in her name	100,0%
Life insurance in her name	100,0%
Savings account in her name	37,2%
Debit card in household	14,7%
Insurance in household	28,5%
Knows about pensions	51,0%
Pension in household	9,3%

Table 1. Source: Own compilation from baseline survey. Figures are highly reliable, as whenever a respondent answered 'yes', she was asked to show documents of proof.

Table 2 provides a test of random assignment to treatment and control groups. In addition, it provides a test of random assignment within the treatment group to female or male trainers. As can be derived from Table 2, the three main baseline indicators used as basis for the randomisation do not vary systematically by treatment or trainer status and neither do the other baseline indicators that may vary with the (potential to improve) financial literacy levels.[19] The only exception to this is the financial services index in the Financial Literacy Intervention panel.[20] Since this is not considered a main predictor of (the potential to change) financial literacy levels, the randomisation is still generally regarded as successful.

---

[19] Note that the average income per capita is statistically significantly different in both tests for random assignment, as well as the median income per capita in the test for random trainer gender allocation. While capita per income is reported as a reference, it does not affect comparability. Samhita employs a strict income policy for issuing loans based on the Samhita Poverty Assessment Score Mechanism, which is more stringent than the global \$1.25 per capita PPP daily expenditure criteria. Nevertheless, average per capita measurements came out relatively high, varying from 250 Rs. per month to Rs. 6,750 per month. This was most probably due to measurement errors at the time of reporting monthly income because many respondents may have indicated monthly revenue, rather than profits. Income per capita should therefore not affect comparability.

[20] I constructed a financial services index by collating scores based on the following five questions: Do you have a savings account in your name? Does anyone in your household have a Debit/ATM card? Does anyone in your household have an insurance policy? Do you know about pensions? Does anyone in your household have a pension? Per question, 'Yes' and 'No' answers were given numerical values of 1 and 2, respectively. The minimum total score was 5, and the maximum 10.

Test of Random Assignment	Financial Literacy Intervention				Trainer Gender Status (Within Treatment Group)			
	Treatment	Control	Difference significant	p-value	Female Trainer	Male Trainer	Difference significant	p-value
Age								
(mean, t-test unequal variances)	34,1	33,6	No	0,501	34,3	34	No	0,67922
Years of schooling								
(median, Wilcoxon test)	0	4	No	0,4697	1	0	No	0,6512
(mean, t-test unequal variances)	3,77	4,05	No	0,484	3,66	3,57	No	0,82504
Savings account?								
(mean)	1,639	1,596			1,635	1,665		
Chi-square			No	0,328			No	0,495
Income / capita								
(median, Wilcoxon test)	1232,5	1200	No	0,1753	1300	1200	Yes, at 1%	0,009879***
(mean, t-test unequal variances)	1478,98	1299,77	Yes, at 5%	0,00469***	1589,65	1426,97	Yes, at 10%	0,05296*
Literacy levels								
(mean)	1,48	1,47			1,48	1,52		
Chi-square			No	0,788			No	0,404
Household size								
(mean, t-test unequal variances)	4,858	4,886	No	0,82911	4,897	4,864	No	0,80645
Financial services index								
(mean, t-test unequal variances)	8,627	8,446	Yes, at 10%	0,08014*	8,69528	8,65678	No	0,7173
Number of observations	501	166			233	236		

Table 2. Source: Own compilation from baseline survey. The p-value columns report p-values of the respective statistical tests for the hypothesis of equality of means / medians between the treatment (female trainer) and control (male trainer) group, as mentioned in the first column. All t-tests are performed assuming unequal variances. This is considered safer than the Student t-test assuming equal variances in case the true population variances really are unequal, and will still give robust results even when the variances of the true population are equal (Ruxton, 2006). For binary variables, where 'yes' corresponds to a value of 1 and 'no' to a value of 2, a Chi-square test is performed (given the large number of observations and slightly more conservative p-values compared to a Fisher Exact test). When distributions are somewhat skewed, a Wilcoxon median test is performed. In these cases t-tests are also reported for comparison purposes. *** indicates that the difference is statistically significant at the 1 percent level, ** at the 5 percent level, and * at the 10 percent level. Note that the total number of observations in the Trainer Status panel equals 469 instead of 501 individuals, as for the trainer gender analysis one treatment group in Arera Colony was dropped.

6. Departures from Perfect Randomisation

The randomised field experiment suffered from both partial compliance and attrition. Paragraphs 6.1 and 6.2 describe how this influenced the internal validity of the results. The analysis concerns the financial literacy intervention only. Paragraph 6.3 discusses how these departures have affected comparability between trainer gender status groups.

6.1 Partial Compliance

The baseline survey reported that 99.5% of the clients were interested in participating in an FLTP. Of these, 222 out of 501 invitees eventually participated in the training programme (44.3%). Compliance in the control group (i.e., completing the pre-test) was 80.7%.[21] Partial compliance is a common issue in randomised field experiments, and even more so in educational interventions since it is difficult to compel participation. This problem is usually tackled by producing an intention-to-treat (ITT) estimate from which a treatment on the treated effect (TOT) can be derived. Ideally, this study would have produced both of these estimates. However, not all projected treatment and control groups have been fully covered by the pre-test (and post-test). Only those who complied with the treatment were requestd to take the tests.[22] This prevents producing an ITT estimate.

As an alternative, this study reduces the sample based on compliance in order to produce a TOT estimate. This reintroduces potentially serious selection biases, in particular when individuals who comply with the intervention have systematically different characteristics compared to those who do not comply. The results may then no longer be representative of all

---

[21] Imperfect compliance (i.e., control group clients receiving the intervention) was not an issue in this experiment.

[22] In treatment groups, the pretest was administered at the beginning of the first session. In control groups, pretests were administered during surprise visits at home. Some control group clients could not be covered due to repeated unavailability at the time of the survey.

of Samhita's urban microfinance clients, let alone a higher level of generalisability.

Keeping these reservations in mind, there is reason to believe that this experiment remains instructive. It gives very accurate estimates of the effect of the intervention on the compliers, as long as control and treatment groups are comparable. As Duflo et al. (2006:51) argue, in some cases it is very valuable to understand the average effect of the intervention itself, rather than that of the ITT. This study is indeed interested in understanding the specific link between financial literacy levels and financial literacy training, rather than the broader policy question of whether financial literacy training policies should be scaled up.

The question then is whether treatment and control groups are sufficiently similar to ensure the internal validity of results. The comparability could be in jeopardy because the treatment groups were invited to participate in the FLTP and were therefore given the choice of showing up for the programme, whereas the control group was not given this choice. The control group was paid a surprise visit at home and given the pre-test. Compliance in the control group therefore depends less on individual choice.

The experiment does not reveal *why* some clients chose not to participate in the training. For example, a client may not have shown up because she perceived the training as too challenging, or quite the contrary, she may have felt that it was not useful for her. Also, clients may have been unavailable simply due to work or they were out of town. If the latter was the case, the bias is likely to be small. In the other cases, however, biased estimators in question (1) become problematic because those factors are most likely correlated with (the potential to improve) initial financial literacy levels. However, it is not obvious in which direction this choice factor could potentially skew the results in this case.

The choice factor may be correlated with observable or unobservable characteristics that influence (the potential to improve) initial financial literacy levels. If the choice factor is correlated with observable characteristics, this should translate into differences in the main baseline indicators between compliers and non-compliers in the treatment group. For example, if those who have a higher educational level, or who already participate in the financial market choose to not participate in the financial literacy training, one would expect to observe a significant difference in the years of schooling or the number of people who have a savings account between these groups. However, this is not the case. When testing the hypotheses of equality of means (medians) of the main baseline indicators between compliers and non-compliers in the treatment group, no systemic differences appear. The same applies in comparing compliers and non-compliers in the control group. The results are reported in Appendix 1.

These results are reinforced when comparing the treatment group compliers to the control group compliers. Comparing both groups on equality of means (medians) of the main baseline indicators gives the following very robust results: All p-values are higher than 0.34.[23] For most indicators, p-values even increased compared to the test of randomisation, which suggests that the variations of the observed characteristics of compliers (both treatment and control) are more homogeneously distributed than in the experimental sample. Moreover, analysing average pre-test scores for complier treatment and control groups also do not reveal statistically significant differences between treatment and control group compliers. Pre-test scores are evenly distributed, which suggests that outliers do not drive this result. This suggests that the main baseline indicators chosen as the basis for randomisation are indeed accurate predictors of financial literacy levels. The results are reported in Table 3.

---

[23] When testing for equality of means (medians) of income per capita, the null hypothesis could be rejected at the 5 (10) percent level.

| | Financial Literacy Intervention | | | |
	Compliers Treatment	Compliers Control	Difference significant	p-value
Age				
(mean, t-test unequal variances)	34,31	33,77	No	0,51709
Years of schooling				
(median, Wilcoxon test)	0	4	No	0,3551
(mean, t-test unequal variances)	3,71	4,18	No	0,34222
Savings account?				
(mean)	1,60811	1,6194		
Chi-square			No	0,832
Income / capita				
(median, Wilcoxon test)	1250	1170,83	Yes, at 10%	0,09998*
(mean, t-test unequal variances)	1449,78	1272,64	Yes, at 5%	0,02199**
Literacy levels				
(mean)	1,46364	1,46269		
Chi-square			No	0,986
Household size				
(mean, t-test unequal variances)	5,0045	4,9403	No	0,66894
Financial services index				
(mean, t-test unequal variances)	8,54505	8,47015	No	0,55334
Number of observations	222	134		

Table 3. Source: Own compilation from baseline survey. The p-value column reports p-values of the respective statistical tests for the hypothesis of equality of means / medians between the compliers treatment and compliers control group, as mentioned in the first column. For a motivation for the respective statistical tests used, see footnote table 2. *** indicates that the difference is statistically significant at the 1 percent level, ** at the 5 percent level, and * at the 10 percent level.

All of the above suggests that despite the partial compliance and presence of a choice factor for the treatment group, the comparability of complier treatment and control groups has not changed significantly for the main baseline indicators and, most importantly, for the initial financial literacy levels. These results only refer to observable characteristics, however. There may still be unobservable factors (such as motivation and interest in financial issues) that differ between complier treatment and control group. While this has not shown up in initial financial literacy levels, this may influence the extent to which participants are able to increase their financial literacy levels and thus remains a potential source of bias.

6.2 Attrition

Another source of potential bias is the differential attrition between treatment and comparison groups.[24] The testing procedure was designed to min-
imise attrition. Participants who attended two or more sessions, but who
were not present at the post-test, were visited at home to administer the
post-test. Control group compliers were revisited if they were not at home
the first time. Table 4 presents the attrition levels and the difference in pre-
test scores between stayers and attriters.[25]

Attrition Financial Literacy Training	Treatment	Control
Financial Literacy Training		
Number of observations	43	32
Percent attrition (after pre-tests)	19%	24%
Pre-test score attritors	2,5349	2,6875
Pre-test score stayers	2,3547	2,3529
Difference in Average Score at Pretest Attriters-Stayers	0,1802	0,3346
t-test mean attriters vs stayers, p-value:	0,37524	0,05162

Table 4. Source: Own compilation. All t-tests are performed assuming
unequal variances.

Attrition was 19% in the treatment group and 24% in the control group.[26]
Differential attrition can affect the internal validity when control and
treatment groups are no longer comparable, i.e., when different types of
people drop out of the respective groups (Angrist, 1996). In terms of financial literacy levels, this does seem to be the case: The attriters have slightly
higher average pre-test scores than stayers in both the treatment and con-

---

[24] Attriters are those who did take a pre-test (i.e. compliers), but not a post-test.

[25] Similar to Banerjee et al. (2005).

[26] Attrition in the treatment group largely comprised participants that only came once
(83.7%).

trol groups. This suggests that the less financially literate participants stayed in the experiment. Keeping in mind, that Cole et al. (2009) found that the training has a modest impact among the relatively uneducated and financially illiterate households (and no impact for the general population at all), this attrition may bias the results obtained from equation (1) upwards.

The question, then, is how large this attrition bias is. When testing the hypothesis of equality of means, average pre-test scores are significantly different for attriters and stayers in the control group, yet not for attriters and stayers in the treatment group. This result is important with respect to the size of the bias. Within the treatment group, the decision to drop out or stay may have been due to insufficient need for the programme, or because of other unobservable factors that correlate with (the potential to increase) initial financial literacy levels. However, insofar as these unobservable factors result in different average pre-test scores, these differences are statistically insignificant. This is also true for the three main baseline indicators.[27] This suggests a very modest bias due to non-random programme dropout. This is supported by observations from the field, in which it appeared that many dropouts were caused by time conflicts between the training timeslots and work or picking up children from school.

Within the control group, attrition does seem to be a potential problem, given its magnitude and the significant difference in average pre-test scores. However, recalling the testing procedure, this seems to be due to a random draw rather than to a systemic bias since staff visits to administer the post-test were unannounced and repeated when the person was not at home the first time. In total, although prudence in interpreting the final results remains imperative, attrition seems unlikely to have had a significant additional effect on the validity of the results.[28] This result is bolstered

---

[27] See also Appendix 2.

[28] Keeping in mind the potential bias due to the different nature of compliance as discussed in paragraph 6.1.

when comparing stayers in treatment and control groups along all the main baseline indicators: All p-values are in excess of 0.16.[29] Most importantly, with a p-value of 0.79755, the difference in average pre-test scores is statistically indistinguishable from zero. The results are reported in Table 5.

| | Financial Literacy Intervention | | | |
	Stayers Treatment	Stayers Control	Difference significant	p-value
Age (mean, t-test unequal variances)	34,39	33,14	No	0,16856
Years of schooling (median, Wilcoxon test)	0	4	No	0,317
(mean, t-test unequal variances)	3,79	4,13	No	0,35414
Savings account? (mean)	1,58659	1,64706		
Chi-square			No	0,318
Income / capita (median, Wilcoxon test)	1200	1170,83	No	0,1622
(mean, t-test unequal variances)	1404,67	1244,91	Yes, at 10%	0,05114*
Literacy levels (mean)	1,46328	1,43137	No	0,67218
Chi-square				
Household size (mean, t-test unequal variances)	5,07263	4,96078	No	0,51592
Financial services index (mean, t-test unequal variances)	8,43575	8,5	No	0,6461
Average pretest score (mean, t-test unequal variances)	2,3547	2,3529	No	0,79755
Number of observations	179	102		

Table 5. Source: Own compilation from baseline survey. The p-value column reports p-values of the respective statistical tests for the hypothesis of equality of means / medians between the compliers treatment and compliers control group, as mentioned in the first column. For a motivation for the respective statistical tests used, see footnote table 2. *** indicates that the difference is statistically significant at the 1 percent level, ** at the 5 percent level, and * at the 10 percent level.

---

[29] An exception to this is the t-test for equality of means for income per capita (p-value = 0.05114).

The remainder of this study analyses the effects of the financial literacy intervention and trainer gender experiment based on stayers only, thereby reducing the sample size to 281 women (of which 179 were in the treatment group, and 102 in the control group). Table 6 summarises the sampling procedure of this study.

Sampling Procedure		
	N	Percent
Baseline surveyed members	9195	100%
Baseline surveyed members selected branches	4153	45%
Of whom, Arera Colony	2359	25,7%
Of whom, Nehru Nagar	1794	19,5%
Experimental Sample	667	7,3%
Treatment Group Assignment	501	5,4%
Of whom, FEMALE Trainer	233	
Of whom, MALE Trainer	236	
Control Group Assignment	166	1,8%
Compliers Sample		
Compliers Treatment, according to Pretest	222	2,4%
Of whom, FEMALE Trainer	94	
Of whom, MALE Trainer	117	
Compliers Control, according to Pretest	134	1,5%
Stayers Sample, for final analysis		
Stayers Treatment, according to Pre- and Posttest	179	1,9%
Of whom, Treatment FEMALE	73	
Of whom, Treatment MALE	96	
Stayers Control, according to Pre- and Posttest	102	1,1%

Table 6. Source: own compilation. When randomly assigning treatment groups into FEMALE and MALE trainer status, one group in Arera Colony was left out, due to an uneven number of groups.

6.3   Effects of Departures from Perfect Randomisation on Comparability by Trainer Gender Status

When focussing on stayers only, neither partial compliance, nor attrition affects the internal validity of the estimators of the trainer gender effect since both trainer gender status groups belong to the stayers within the financial literacy treatment group. All the participants were likely to share similar unobservable characteristics (choice factor in particular) with respect to treatment participation.

Analysing the observable characteristics of stayers by trainer gender status gives improved results compared to the earlier test of randomisation: All differences in means (medians) on baseline indicators are statistically indistinguishable from zero and report high p-values. The results are reported in Table 7.

| | Trainer Gender Status (Within Stayers Treatment Group) | | | |
	Female Trainer	Male Trainer	Difference significant	p-value
Age (mean, t-test unequal variances)	34,07	34,73	No	0,58588
Years of schooling (median, Wilcoxon test)	0	0	No	0,794
(mean, t-test unequal variances)	3,78082	3,52083	No	0,71426
Savings account? (mean)	1,57534	1,59375		
Chi-square			No	0,81
Income / capita (median, Wilcoxon test)	1250	1200	No	0,2435
(mean, t-test unequal variances)	1454	1409,56	No	0,69683
Literacy levels (mean)	1,48611	1,436311	No	0,7704
Chi-square				
Household size (mean, t-test unequal variances)	5,09589	5,07292	No	0,91798
Financial services index (mean, t-test unequal variances)	8,45205	8,47917	No	0,88148
Average pretest score (mean, t-test unequal variances)	2,054796	2,55208	Yes, at 1%	0,00344
Number of observations	73	96		

Table 7. Source: Own compilation from baseline survey. The p-value column reports p-values of the respective statistical tests for the hypothesis of equality of means / medians between the compliers treatment and compliers control group, as mentioned in the first column. For a motivation for the respective statistical tests used, see footnote table 2. *** indicates that the difference is statistically significant at the 1 percent level, ** at the 5 percent level, and * at the 10 percent level.

Strikingly, when comparing the average pre-test scores by trainer gender status, a statistically significant difference at the 1% level appears. This is remarkable since both groups share similar variations in the characteristics that are regarded as predictors for financial literacy levels (i.e., the main baseline indicators). There are three plausible explanations for this result. Differential financial literacy levels by trainer gender status could be a result of either:

1. Observable characteristics that differ systematically between the two subgroups;
2. Random probability in draw from sampling distribution;
3. Unobservable characteristics that differ systematically between the two subgroups.

As already shown in Table 7, observable characteristics do not seem to explain this result since the tests of equality of means (medians) report very high p-values on all indicators. The outcome could also simply be the result of a random draw from the underlying sampling distribution: The compliers treatment group. Although this is possible, it seems more likely that an unobservable factor is at work, which is not captured in the main observable indicators since the difference appears to be systemic.

Luckily, this pre-existing difference can be accounted for by estimating a difference-in-difference estimator. This is possible because pre-test and post-test data exists for the financial literacy levels based on treatment status. Assuming that in the absence of the treatment, both groups would have followed parallel trends in terms of financial literacy development, the unbiased estimate of the treatment effect can be estimated by the following simple specification (See also Duflo et al., 2006:12):

$$\Delta FinLiteracy_i = \alpha + \beta * FemaleTrainer + \varepsilon_i \tag{3}$$

Where $\Delta FinLiteracy_i$ is the change in average financial literacy levels, and *FemaleTrainer* is a dummy for assignment to a female trainer. This specification is estimated in the following section.

7. Results

This section reports the experimental results for both the financial literacy intervention and the trainer gender experiment. When interpreting results, it is important to keep in mind that results concern the stayers sample only. For the possible biases that may result from this, see the previous section.

7.1 Financial Literacy Intervention

The FLTP, as conducted by Samhita, appears to have a very significant effect on the participants' average financial literacy levels. The difference in average financial literacy scores for the pre-tests and post-tests for stayers in the treatment group is significant at the 1% level. Table 8 tabulates this result in addition to presenting disaggregated scores per question. Scores improved significantly for the three standardised questions based on Lusardi and Mitchell (2006), but not for question four.

Measured Financial Literacy, Stayers Treatment Group		Pretest	Posttest	Difference significant	p-value
1. Compound Interest	% Correct	72,6%	86,6%	Yes, at 1%	0,001***
2. If savings earns 1% and inflation is 2%, after one year is buying power greater, less or the same?	% Correct	73,7%	84,9%	Yes, at 5%	0,013**
3. Is a bank safer for savings than an agent?	% Correct	40,8%	77,7%	Yes, at 1%	0***
4. Borrowing Rs. 500, repaying Rs. 600 versus repaying 15 %	% Correct	51,4%	54,8%	No	0,525
Question 1 and 2 taken together	% Correct	49,2%	73,2%	Yes, at 1%	0,00004***
Question 1, 2 and 3 taken together	% Correct	24,6%	57,0%	Yes, at 1%	0***
All four questions taken together	% Correct	17,3%	33,0%	Yes, at 1%	0***
Mean share of correct answers question 1,2 and 3		62,4%	83,1%		
Mean share of correct answers all four questions		59,6%	76,0%		
All questions taken together	Avg. Score (out of 4)	2,385475	3,03911	Yes, at 1%	0***
Number of oberservations		179	179		

Table 8. Source: Own compilation from pre- and posttests. The p-value column reports p-values of a Chi-square tests, as it concerns binary variables: an answer can be either 'right' or 'wrong'. *** indicates that the difference is statistically significant at the 1 percent level, ** at the 5 percent level, and * at the 10 percent level.

These results are derived from looking at the treatment group only.[30] Although this gives a fair initial indication of the effect of the FLTP, it does not reveal much about the magnitude of the effect. Also, it does not fully exclude the possibility that factors other than the FLTP may have affected financial literacy levels during the time in which the training took place.

---

[30]   For a similar methodology, see Bertrand and Mullainathan (2004).

Therefore, causal inference cannot be firmly established on the basis of the results of the treatment group alone. To obtain estimates of the *causal* effect, therefore, equation (1) is estimated. This includes control group data. These results are presented in Table 9.

	FinLiteracy
LitTraining	0.686***
	(0.112)
constant	2.353***
	(0.090)
SampleSize	281
AdjR-squared	0.115
* $p<0.05$, ** $p<0.01$, *** $p<0.001$	

Table 9. Source: Own compilation from post-tests.

The point estimate on LitTraining in equation (1) is large and statistically significant. This confirms the previous result and suggests that the FLTP has a considerable effect on participants' initial financial literacy level. A participant in the training programme is likely to increase her average financial literacy level by an average score of 0.69 out of 4. This is equivalent to 17.25%.

7.2 Trainer Gender Effects

Testing the possibility that trainer gender affects learning outcomes do not result in a significant effect, when estimating equation (2), the point estimate on FemaleTrainer is negative, but, statistically insignificant. Remarkably, when estimating equation (3), accounting for the difference in the pre-tests by trainer gender status, the point estimate on FemaleTrainer switches signs and turns positive. This suggests that the pre-test scores are an omitted variable in equation (2). This is not remarkable given the significantly lower average pre-test scores for participants trained by a female. However, the result remains insignificant. This suggests that trainer gender status does not significantly affect learning outcomes in this experiment. The results are reported in Table 10.

	FinLiteracy	dFinLiteracy
FemaleTrainer	-0.176	0.321
	(0.136)	(0.203)
constant	3.094***	0.542***
	(0.089)	(0.133)
SampleSize	169	169
AdjR-squared	0.004	0.009
* p<0.05, ** p<0.01, *** p<0.001		

Table 10. Source: Own compilation from pre-tests and post-tests.

Analysing trainer evaluations by comparing cumulative ratings by trainer gender, a small systemic trend in learning perceptions can be detected. Comparing questions that are associated with self-recognition and class comfort does not reveal a substantial difference in learning perceptions by trainer gender. However, when comparing trainer evaluation questions associated with perceptions of subject authority, the perceptions of male trainers slightly outstrip those of the female trainers systematically. Figures 1–4 below show this trend:

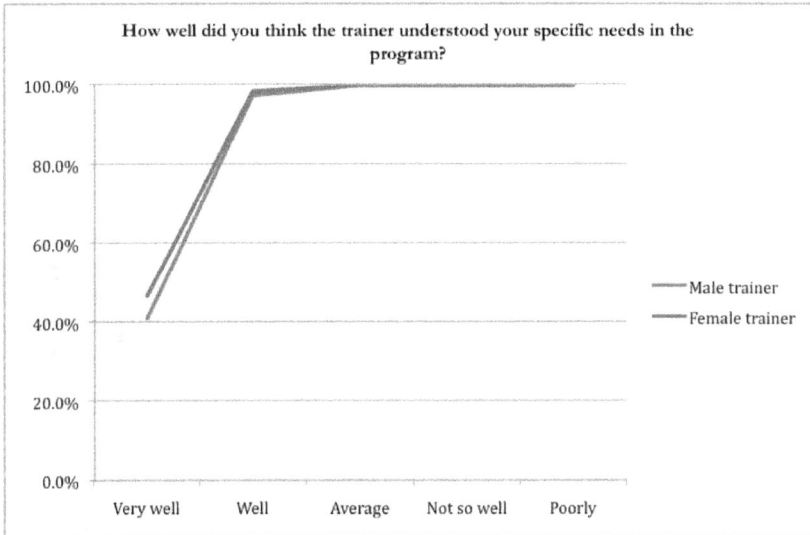

How well did you think the trainer understood your specific needs in the program?

Figure 1. Source: Own Compilation. (Note: percentages are cumulative).

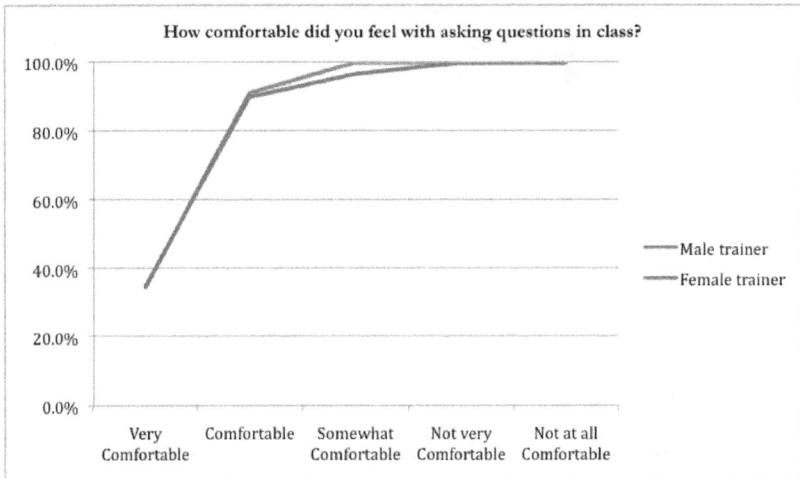

How comfortable did you feel with asking questions in class?

Figure 2. Source: Own Compilation. (Note: percentages are cumulative).

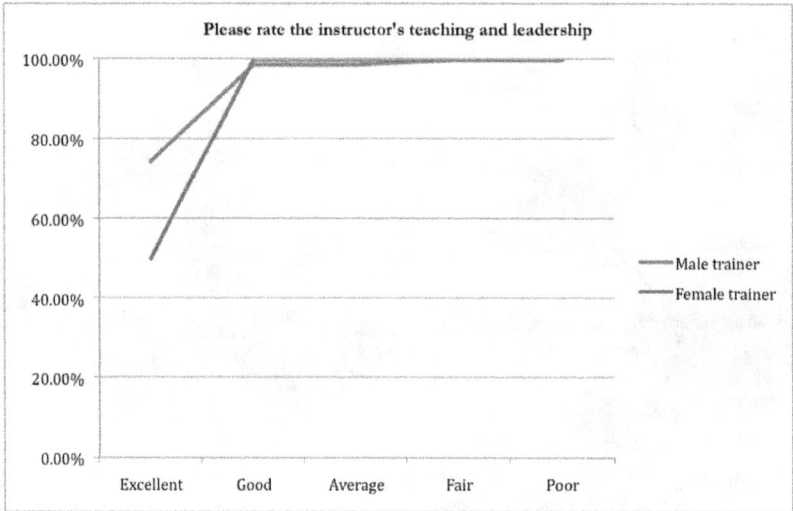

Figure 3. Source: Own Compilation. (Note: percentages are cumulative).

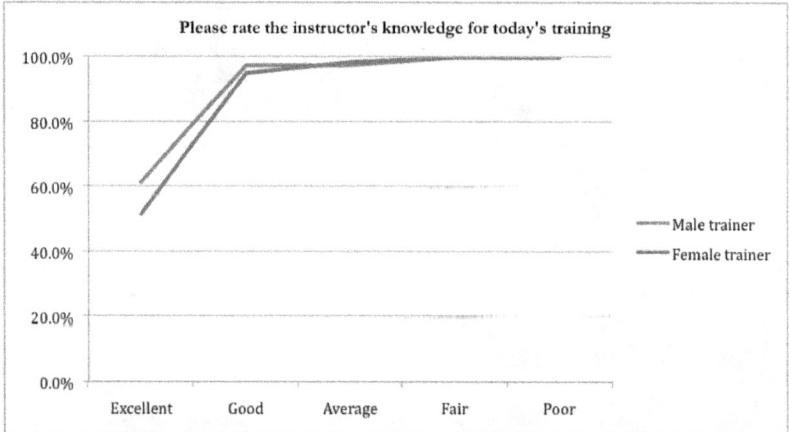

Figure 4. Source: Own Compilation. (Note: percentages are cumulative).

8. Discussion

8.1 Financial Literacy Intervention

The results of the experiment show that an FLTP for urban microfinance clients positively affects average financial literacy levels. Combining this finding with earlier research on the correlation between financial literacy and a household's wellbeing suggests that the increase in financial literacy levels found in this study, as a result of the FLTP, would result in an increased demand for welfare enhancing financial services. This suggests a conclusion that is quite different from the previous experiments on financial literacy training is possible. Cole et al. (2009) concluded that financial literacy training is hardly beneficial because it does not significantly increase the demand for financial services. This study, however, has shown that an FLTP is beneficial because it can raise financial literacy levels.

Two possibilities follow from this: Either the financial literacy training of Cole et al. (2009) was unsuccessful in raising financial literacy levels, or maybe it was successful, but, as they point out, external constraints rather than limited financial literacy could explain the low financial services uptake found in their study. To be able to exclude either one of these possibilities, a follow-up study of the findings of my experiment needs to be done, in order to see whether higher financial literacy levels translate into higher financial services uptake.[31] If this is the case, the findings in this study would contradict Cole et al. (2009). This, in turn, would constitute a reason to continue and improve the practice of conducting FLTPs as a part of development programmes. If a follow-up study does not result in higher financial services uptake, it would support the findings of Cole et al.

---

[31] Time constraints prevented such follow-up; this would be the starting point for further research.

(2009). This would then point to the necessity of removing external constraints.

The positive outcome of the experiment in this study only holds if alternative interpretations of the results can be excluded. There is a possibility that the financial literacy measurement does not accurately capture the financial literacy levels of the chosen population. Although this paper has used the best methods available, this does not mean they are fool proof. The questions used to measure financial literacy are heavily geared towards testing mathematical financial skills. While mathematical skills are important, there is more to financial literacy than calculation. The poor may be financially illiterate, but this does not prevent them from being clever about money. As Duflo aptly puts it, 'they are "incredibly smart" about day-to-day financial matters, "because the cost of errors is much bigger", but "so busy doing this effort, and optimizing on some margin, that they might entirely miss some huge elephant in the room," like the importance of buying fertilizer for their crops, or immunizing their children' (Quoted in Parker 2010). Expressed differently, understanding the value of putting your money into a savings account, rather than keeping it under the mattress, is an expression of financial literacy that does not require calculation. Perhaps the key question here is how to define financial literacy in terms of financial capability when considering the poor. This suggests that more work needs to be done in defining and measuring financial literacy in such a way that it captures forms of financial competences beyond mathematical and financial skills.

8.2 Trainer Gender Experiment

The experimental results show no significant effect of trainer gender on learning outcomes, suggesting that it does not matter whether male or female trainers are employed. This result supports earlier findings by Sabbe and Aelterman (2007), who emphasised that research to date, has found little, if any effect of gender on learning outcomes. However, this study found some evidence that trainer gender affects learning perceptions. In particular, it found that subject authority perceptions are slightly higher for male trainers. This is also consistent with earlier findings, in which there was a small degree of evidence that trainer gender affects learning perceptions (Sabbe & Aelterman, 2007:527). It should be kept in mind, however, that the trend shown in this study is based on relatively small differences between subjective ratings of 'excellent' and 'good'. Surprisingly, no differential effects appear with regard to self-recognition and class comfort. Over 90% of the participants, who had both male and female trainers reported that they felt (very) comfortable in class with asking questions, and over 97% reported that the trainer understood their specific needs (very) well. The participants seemed to be very satisfied with the training overall, which may have eclipsed the evaluations of trainer gender effects in this case.

These results suggest that Samhita should continue using both female and male trainers. Samhita's preference for female trainers is not necessarily justified by wanting to improve learning impact alone. Again, the conclusions of this study are based on the observations of just two pairs of comparable teachers, with highly satisfied training participants. Although this is not an exceptional research setting,[32] a more comparative study between male and female trainers is needed to better understand the general patterns in trainer gender perceptions and outcomes in a development context.

Like in the case of the financial literacy intervention, the findings regarding the effects of trainer gender as presented above only hold provided that the perceptions are measured accurately.[33] Although the measurement is designed on the basis of a coherent theoretical gender framework, it does

---

[32] 'It is not unusual to see a study with samples of one or two teachers' (Sabbe & Aelterman, 2007:528).

[33] For learning outcomes, the same reservations with regard to financial literacy measurements apply as those discussed in subsection 8.1.

not fully exclude the possibility of measuring perceptions that go beyond trainer gender, such as personal characteristics. When interpreting trainer gender perceptions, prudence is therefore essential. The potential biases have been limited, however, by hiring the most comparable set of trainers from the available pool.

8.3 Validity of results: possible pitfalls

8.3.1 Internal Validity

The validity of results in a randomised field experiment strongly relies on the comparability of treatment and control groups (Duflo et al., 2006:8). As discussed extensively in section 6, partial compliance and attrition have potentially reintroduced a selection bias within the experimental sample. In particular, the fact that randomisation was based on baseline characteristics, and not pre-tests, prevented eliminating the choice factor of whether to participate in the financial literacy training or not. The choice factor that was present in treatment groups, but not in control groups, may have split the assigned treatment group along unobservable characteristics that could be correlated with the potential to increase financial literacy levels. This may have resulted in the heterogeneous variation in the unobservable factors between treatment and control groups. This variation is not heterogeneous between compliers and non-compliers, and stayers and attriters, respectively, with regard to the observables, 'years of schooling', 'previous financial market participation' and 'age'. This means that there are good reasons to believe that the direction of the results holds. The magnitude, however, should be interpreted with care.

8.3.2 External Validity

There are three dimensions for the external validity of a randomised evaluation, which are as follows: Whether a program was implemented with special care; how specific the sample is; and how specific the programme is to the context in which the randomised evaluation took place (Duflo et al., 2006:70). In this study, the last two dimensions are of particular concern.

The specificity of the stayers sample, limits the generalisability of the results to the whole experimental sample as originally selected for the randomisation. The results do not necessarily hold for those who did not comply with the treatment. The partial compliance encountered in this study, however, is not exceptional;. in any training program, some degree of partial compliance is likely to be present. In that respect, results may still be instructive for judging the effects of FLTPs on financial literacy levels.

Even if the results hold for the experimental sample, the question is to what extent this sample is representative for Samhita's urban microfinance population. As discussed in subsection 5.1, selection of the experimental sample is random. There is no reason to believe that branch selection was endogenous to the clients' financial literacy levels. Lastly, the question to consider is to what extent Samhita's urban microfinance population is representative of urban microfinance clients across India. Since microfinance institutions mainly target similar groups of the poor, results could be relevant for other microfinance clients as well. However, the specific district context of Madhya Pradesh has to be kept in mind when interpreting the results. The results may be less instructive for poor non-microfinance populations in India since these populations are less likely to be financially experienced, or more importantly, to include males.

Closely related to the specificity of the sample is the specificity of the programme. Possible programme variations are infinite; however, this does not preclude deriving implications for future FLTPs. The significant effect on participants' average financial literacy levels suggests that the content of the programme is educative. In addition, the trainer gender experiment revealed that trainer gender does not significantly affect learning outcomes. On the other hand, a different training frequency, such as one session per week, instead of two, could improve attendance. Although this has not been tested empirically, the relatively low compliance with the treatment (and the reasons mentioned) suggests that this could greatly improve the reach of the training.

Further research would ideally evaluate the impact of the FLTPs by comparing various populations (both microfinance and non-microfinance), and various versions of the programme. Only then, could claims of the replicability of the training programme effects be made. The principal merit of this study lies in further testing two of the theoretical frameworks that underpin FLTPs and gender difference in teaching. Testing these theories in a different context would provide further evidence of the benefits of financial literacy training programmes. Furthermore, this study adds a new chapter to the gender debate in the research on teaching.

9. Conclusion

This study has, to the best of my knowledge, been a first exploration of the specific link between financial literacy training and financial literacy levels within the broader field of research into the causal mechanism between financial literacy and a household's well-being. It provides empirical evidence that a carefully designed financial literacy training programme for microfinance clients in Bhopal increased the average financial literacy scores of the participants. In addition, it found that trainer gender does not affect learning outcomes significantly, but does affect learning perceptions, i.e., perceived subject authority is slightly higher for male trainers than for female trainers.

The data gathered for this study could be further explored with respect to heterogeneous treatment effects. For example, the data could be tested to see whether the increase in financial literacy varies by years of schooling, previous financial market participation or wealth. This goes beyond the purpose of this study, but could help to understand the dynamics of furthering financial literacy better. In addition, whether the impact of a financial literacy training programme varies for different initial financial literacy levels could also be explored (i.e., if those slightly less financially literate experience a greater impact from the training). Finally, the data could generate interesting comparative case study material with regard to Cole et al. (2009), by studying the financial literacy levels of different segments of the poor in India.

By studying the causal mechanism between financial literacy and a household's well-being, this study has focused on microfinance clients in Bhopal. A next step would be to repeat this study for other financial literacy training programmes in developing countries and to devise better ways of measuring the financial capabilities of the poor. Such research, like this study, could be a stepping stone for improving financial literacy training programmes that cater to the needs of the poor.

References

Angrist, J. (1996), *Conditioning on the Probability of Selection to Control Selection Bias*, NBER Technical Paper No. 181.

ATISG, (2010), *Innovative Financial Inclusion, Principles and Report on Innovative Financial Inclusion from the Access through Innovation Sub-Group of the G20 Financial Inclusion.* Retrieved From www.microfinancegateway.org/gm/.../Innovative_Financial_I nclusion.pdf. Accessed on 2nd August, 2010, 13:00 PM.

Banerjee, A., Cole, S., Duflo, E., Linden, L. (2005), *Remedying Education: Evidence from Two Randomized Experiments in India*, NBER Working Paper No. 11904.

Chen, S., Ravaillon, M. (2008), *The Developing World Is Poorer Than We Thought, But No Less Successful in the Fight against Poverty*, World Bank Policy Research Working Paper 4703.

Claessens, S. (2006), 'Access to Financial Services: A Review of the Issues and Public Policy Objectives', *The World Bank Research Observer*, 21(2), pp. 207–240.

Cohen, D., Soto, M. (2007), 'Growth and human capital: good data, good results', *Journal of Economic Growth,* 12, pp.51–76.

Cole, S., Sampson, T. Zia, B. (2009), *Money or Knowledge? What drives demand for financial services in emerging markets?,* Harvard Business School Working paper No. 09–117.

Demirgüç-Kunt, A., Beck, T., Honohan, P. (2008), 'Finance for All?' *World Bank Policy Research Report,* Washington, DC: The World Bank.

Demirgüç-Kunt, A., Beck, T., Soledad Martinez, M. (2007), 'Reaching out: Access to and use of banking services across countries', *Journal of Financial Economics* 85, pp. 234–266.

Duflo, E., Glennerster, R., Kremer, M. (2006), *Using Randomization in Development Economics Research: A Toolkit*, NBER Technical Working Paper No. 333.

Lusardi, A., Mitchell, O. (2006), *Financial Literacy and Planning: Implications for Retirement Wellbeing*, Pension Research Council Working Paper No.1.

Lusardi, A., Mitchell, O., Curto, V. (2009), *Financial Literacy Among the Young: Evidence and Implications for Consumer Policy*, NBER Working Paper No. 15352.

Karlan, D., (2010) 'Helping the poor save more'. *Standford Social Innovation Review*, Winter 2010.

Kempson, E., Whyley, C., Caskey, J., Collard, S. (2000), 'In or Out? Financial Exclusion: A Literature and Research Review', *Consumer Research Report 3*, London: Financial Services Authority.

Menon, P., Deolalikar, A., Bhaskar, A. (2009), *India State Hunger Index, Comparisons of Hunger Across States*, Washington, DC: IFPRI, Bonn; Welt Hunger Hilfe, Riverside: University of California.

Murdoch, j. (1999), 'The Microfinance Promise', Journal of Economic Literature, 37(4), pp. 1569–1614.

Li, Q. (1999), 'Teachers' Beliefs and Gender Differences in Mathematics: A Review', *Educational Research*, 41(1), pp. 63–76.

Parker, I. (2010), 'The Poverty Lab: Transforming development economics, one experiment at a time.' *The New Yorker*, May 17th.

Przeworski, A. (2004), Institutions Matter?, *Government and Opposition*, 39(4), pp.527–40.

Ravaillon, M. (2009), 'Should the Randomistas Rule?', *The Berkeley Electronic Press*, February.

Rodrik, D. (2008), *The New Development Economics: We Shall Experiment, But How Shall We Learn?*, HKS Working Paper No. RWP08–055.

Ruxton, G. (2006), 'The Unequal Variance T-test is an Underused Alterative to Student's T-test and the Mann-Whitney U Test', Behavioral Ecology, pp.688–690.

Sabbe, E., Aelterman, A. (2007), 'Gender in Teaching: A Literature Review', *Teachers and Teaching*, 13(5), pp.521–538.

Van Rooij, M. Lusardi, A., Alessie, R. (2009), *Financial Literacy and Retirement Planning in the Netherlands*, DNB Working Paper No. 231.

Warwick, D., Jatoi, H. (1994), 'Teacher Gender and Student Achievement in Pakistan', *Comparative Education Review*, 38(3), pp.377–399.

Other sources

UNDP multidimensional poverty index
http://hdr.undp.org/en/reports/global/hdr2010/news/title,20523,en.html
Accessed on 30th July, 2010, 15:30PM

http://www.wijzeringeldzaken.nl/english.aspx
Accessed on 2nd August, 2010, 12:00PM

http://www.rbi.org.in/scripts/PublicationDraftReports.aspx?ID=526
Accessed on 2nd August, 2010, 12:00PM

Appendix 1

	Financial Literacy Intervention				Financial Literacy Intervention			
	Compliers Treatment	Non-Compliers Treatment	Difference significant	p-value	Compliers Control	Non-Compliers Control	Difference significant	p-value
Age (mean, t-test unequal variances)	34,31	33,93	No	0,59573	33,77	33	No	0,69761
Years of schooling (median, Wilcoxon test)	0	1	No	0,7347	4	3	No	0,5555
(mean, t-test unequal variances)	3,71	3,82	No	0,78433	4,18	3,4	No	0,38757
Savings account? (mean)	1,60811	1,56308			1,6194	1,5		
Chi-square			No	0,203			No	0,216
Income / capita (median, Wilcoxon test)	-250	1207,142857	No	0,8701	1170,83	1413,37	No	0,23881
(mean, t-test unequal variances)	1449,78	1532,47	No	0,50415	1272,64			
Literacy levels (mean)	1,46364	1,4964			1,46269	1,5		
Chi-square			No	0,467			No	0,705
Household size (mean, t-test unequal variances)	5,0045	4,74194	Yes, at 5%	0,0388**	4,9403	4,65625	No	0,36804
Financial services index (mean, t-test unequal variances)	8,54505	8,69176	No	0,15995	8,47015	8,32375	No	0,57255
Number of observations	222	279			134	32		

Appendix 1. Source: Own compilation from baseline survey. The p value columns report p-values of the respective statistical tests for the hypothesis of equality of means / medians between the treatment and control group, as mentioned in the first column. For a motivation for the respective statistical tests used, see footnote table 2. *** indicates that the difference is statistically significant at the 1 percent level, ** at the 5 percent level, and * at the 10 percent level.

Appendix 2

	Financial Literacy Intervention				Financial Literacy Intervention			
	Stayers Treatment	Attriters Treatment	Difference significant	p-value	Stayers Control	Attriters Control	Difference significant	p-value
Age (mean, t-test unequal variances)	34,39	33,98	No	0,77468	33,14	35,78	No	0,11607
Years of schooling (median, Wilcoxon test)	0	2	No	0,7722	4	0	No	0,4992
(mean, t-test unequal variances)	3,79	3,37	No	0,55235	4,13	3,75	No	0,54641
Savings account? (mean)	1,58659	1,69767			1,64706	1,53125		
Chi-square			No	0,18			No	0,297
Income / capita (median, Wilcoxon test)	1200	1333,33	No	0,2679	1170,83	1183,33333	No	0,5945
(mean, t-test unequal variances)	1404,67	1637,58	No	0,14723	1244,91	1361,01146	No	0,43066
Literacy levels (mean)	1,46328	1,46512			1,43137	1,5625		
Chi-square			No	0,982			No	0,226
Household size (mean, t-test unequal variances)	5,07263	4,72093	No	0,14126	4,96078	4,875	No	0,74759
Financial services index (mean, t-test unequal variances)	8,43575	9	Yes, at 1%	0,00195***	8,5	8,375	No	0,62867
Number of observations	179	43			102	32		

Appendix 2. Source: Own compilation from baseline survey. The p-value columns report p-values of the respective statistical tests for the hypothesis of equality of means / medians between the treatment and control group, as mentioned in the first column. For a motivation for the respective statistical tests used, see footnote table 2. *** indicates that the difference is statistically significant at the 1 percent level, ** at the 5 percent level, and * at the 10 percent level.

UNIVERSITY MEETS MICROFINANCE

edited by PlaNet Finance Deutschland e.V.

ISSN 2190-2291

ibidem-Verlag

Melchiorstr. 15

D-70439 Stuttgart

info@ibidem-verlag.de

www.ibidem-verlag.de
www.ibidem.eu
www.edition-noema.de
www.autorenbetreuung.de

www.ingramcontent.com/pod-product-compliance
Lightning Source LLC
Chambersburg PA
CBHW070410200326
41518CB00011B/2146